Meet the Dinosaurs!: When Reptiles Ruled

Meet the Plant-Eating Dinosaurs

by Rebecca Donnelly
illustrated by Alan Brown

Grasshopper

Tools for Parents & Teachers

Grasshopper Books enhance imagination and introduce the earliest readers to fiction with fun storylines and illustrations. The easy-to-read text supports early reading experiences with repetitive sentence patterns and sight words.

Before Reading

- Discuss the cover illustration. What do they see?
- Look at the glossary together. Discuss the words.

Read the Book

- Read the book to the child, or have him or her read independently.
- "Walk" through the book and look at the illustrations. What is happening in the story?

After Reading

- Prompt the child to think more. Ask: There were many plant-eating dinosaurs. What herbivores do you know of that live today? Do you know what kind of plants they eat?

Grasshopper Books are published by Jump!
5357 Penn Avenue South
Minneapolis, MN 55419
www.jumplibrary.com

Library of Congress Cataloging-in-Publication Data

Names: Donnelly, Rebecca, author.
Brown, Alan, illustrator.
Title: Meet the plant-eating dinosaurs / Rebecca Donnelly; illustrated by Alan Brown.
Description: Minneapolis, MN: Jump!, Inc., [2022]
Series: Meet the dinosaurs!: when reptiles ruled
Includes index.
Audience: Ages 7-10
Identifiers: LCCN 2021037981 (print)
LCCN 2021037982 (ebook)
ISBN 9781636906140 (hardcover)
ISBN 9781636906157 (paperback)
ISBN 9781636906164 (ebook)
Subjects: LCSH: Dinosaurs–Food–Juvenile literature.
Herbivores–Juvenile literature.
Classification: LCC QE861.5 .D6846 2022 (print)
LCC QE861.5 (ebook)
DDC 567.9–dc23
LC record available at https://lccn.loc.gov/2021037981
LC ebook record available at https://lccn.loc.gov/2021037982

Editor: Eliza Leahy
Direction and Layout: Anna Peterson
Illustrator: Alan Brown

Printed in the United States of America at Corporate Graphics in North Mankato, Minnesota.

Table of Contents

Plant Power

Hi! I'm Mona the Mamenchisaurus. I'm an herbivore. That means I eat plants. Some plant-eating dinosaurs are small. Others are big, like me.

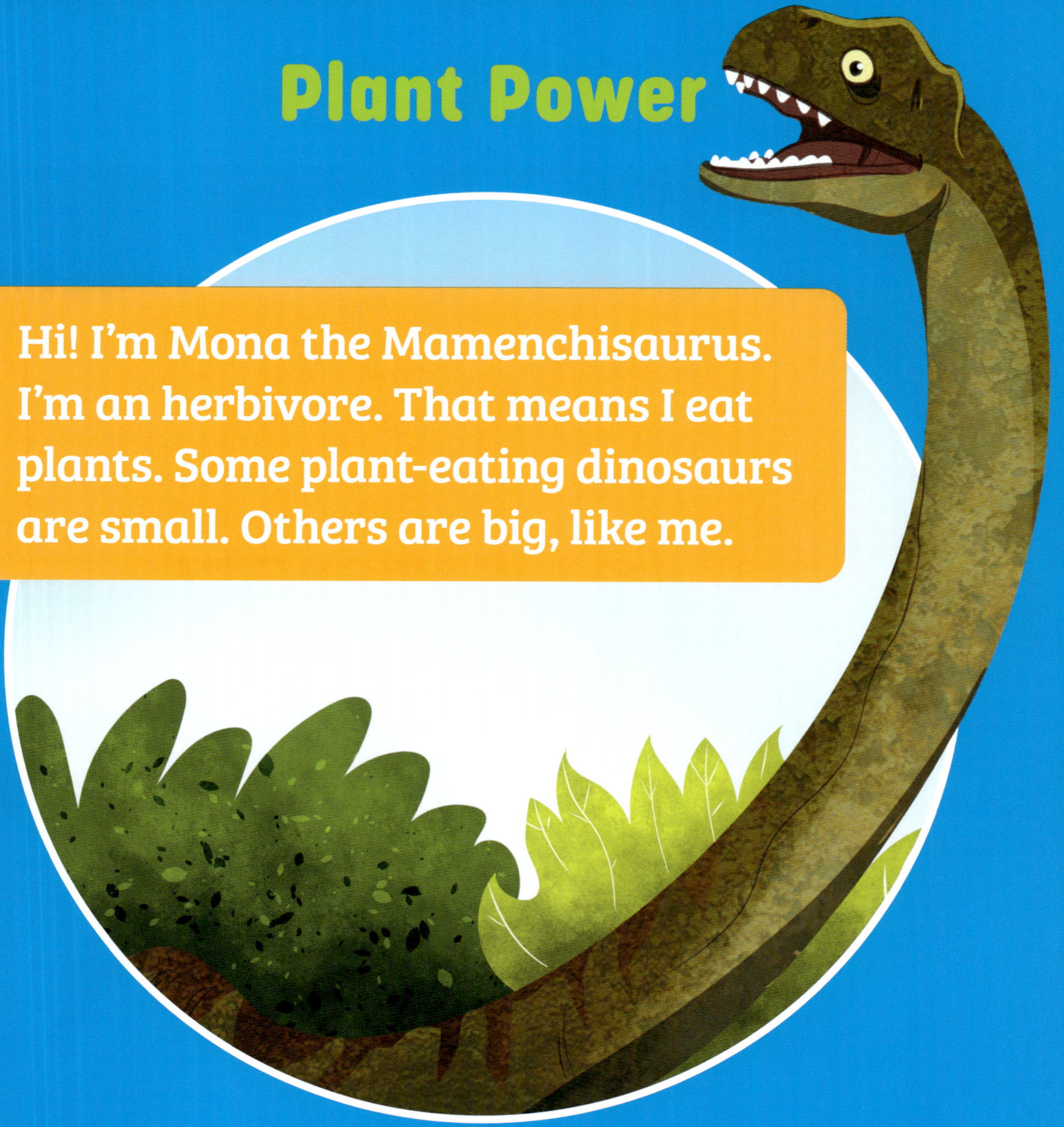

My neck is 30 feet (9.1 meters) long. I can stand in one place and move my neck in all directions to eat. Come meet some other plant-eating dinosaurs!

I’m Tanner the Triceratops. My horns and frill help me attract a mate, but I can use them to fight other Triceratops if I need to! My frill protects my neck.

My beak-like mouth helps me grasp tough plants. My favorites are ferns and palms.

frill
horn
mouth

I'm Aiden the Apatosaurus. I'm one of the biggest herbivores. I'm 69 feet (21 m) long. That's longer than a semitruck!

I love to eat ferns. I don't chew them with my teeth, though. I swallow them whole. *Gulp!*

I'm Nick the Nothronychus. At 12 feet (3.7 m) tall, I'm shorter than some of these other herbivores, but I can reach high with my arms. I hook my claws on tree branches to pull them close. Then I chomp on the leaves!

claw

Hi, I'm Petra the Plateosaurus. I stand on my strong hind legs and stretch my neck to eat leaves. My wide, flat teeth chew them up.

I have a powerful bite, so predators better watch out!

I'm Pat the Parasaurolophus. Standing on my hind legs, I can reach pine needles and leaves. I run fast. If a predator chases me, I can run 25 miles (40 kilometers) per hour!

When I make noise, the sound bounces around inside my crest. My friends and family can hear it from far away!

crest

Hey, I'm Alice. I'm an Ankylosaurus. I'm 23 feet (7.0 m) long. Like many herbivores, I have to defend myself against predators. My armor helps!

If a T. rex gets close, I use the club on my tail to fight!

I'm Spencer the Stegosaurus. I have a club on my tail, too, but mine has spikes! It's called a thagomizer. Like Alice, I use it to defend myself from predators.

The plates on my back aren't armor. They make me look good so I can attract a mate!

plate

I'm Ava the Albertadromeus, one of the smallest herbivorous dinosaurs. I'm only 30 pounds (14 kilograms). Lots of predators want to eat small dinosaurs like me. It's a good thing I'm a fast runner!

Dinosaurs are extinct now, but we were pretty amazing when we ruled the planet!

predator

Timeline

Dinosaurs lived millions of years ago. Take a look at when the dinosaurs in this book lived!

Mamenchisaurus
(mah-men-chi-SORE-us)

225 MILLION YEARS AGO (MYA) 200 175 150

TRIASSIC PERIOD
252–200 MYA

JURASSIC PERIOD
199–145 MYA

Plateosaurus
(plat-ee-oh-SORE-us)

Apatosaurus
(ah-PAT-oh-sore-us)

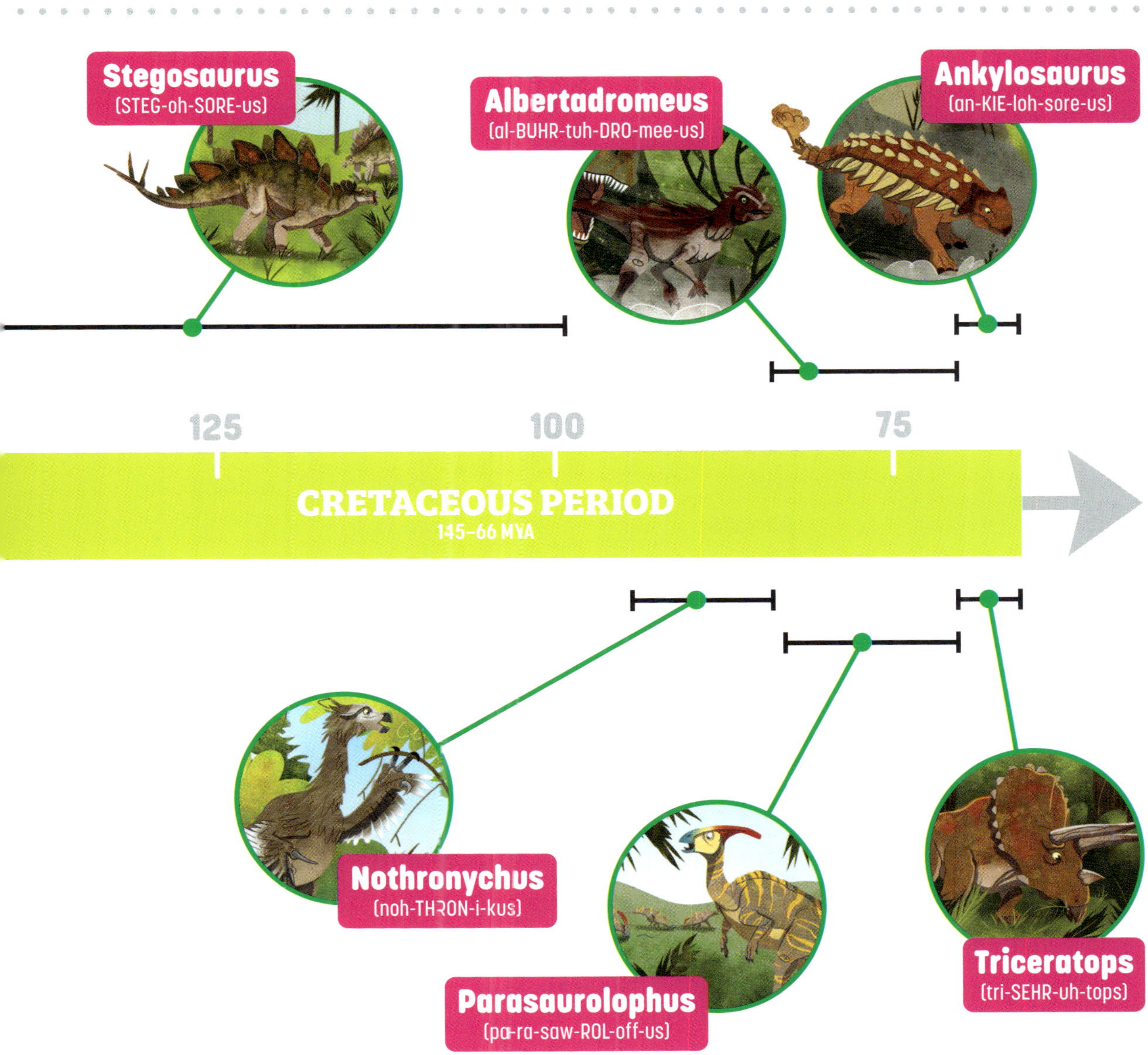

Stegosaurus
(STEG-oh-SORE-us)
Albertadromeus
(al-BUHR-tuh-DRO-mee-us)
Ankylosaurus
(an-KIE-loh-sore-us)
125
100
75
CRETACEOUS PERIOD
145–66 MYA
Nothronychus
(noh-THRON-i-kus)
Parasaurolophus
(pa-ra-saw-ROL-off-us)
Triceratops
(tri-SEHR-uh-tops)

Glossary

armor: A hard covering that protects the body.

attract: To get something's interest.

defend: To protect from harm.

extinct: No longer found alive and known about only through fossils or history.

herbivore: An animal that eats plants.

hind: Back or rear.

mate: One member of a breeding pair of animals.

predators: Animals that hunt other animals for food.

Index

To Learn More

FACT SURFER

Finding more information is as easy as 1, 2, 3.

1. Go to www.factsurfer.com
2. Enter "**meettheplant-eatingdinosaurs**" into the search box.
3. Choose your book to see a list of websites.